A Cutting-Edge School of Ministry
Student Manual on Kingdom Living and
The Emerging King-Priest Leadership Paradigm

By

Dr. Francis Myles
Chancellor
www.francismylesacademy.com

Editing and Graphic Design by Karen Hosey

A MESSAGE FROM THE CHANCELLOR

The Beginning...

When I wrote the book <u>The Order of Melchizedek</u>, I underestimated the level of hunger that existed in the Body of Christ for a book about an ancient priestly order. An Order that has present-day ramifications for followers of Christ who are tired of "church as usual" and knowing Christ "the image of the invisible God" from a religiously safe distance. By far, my biggest shock came from seeing how many marketplace leaders and ministers (businessmen and women) went into a frenzy of delight when they got a copy of the book. Within months of this book's release, many businessmen and women were affectionately calling <u>The Order of Melchizedek</u> their "Marketplace Bible." Things quickly went over the top for me when pastors joined marketplace leaders in celebrating this book. One great man of God who presides over 200 churches, told me that <u>The Order of Melchizedek</u> is the best book that he has ever read in 40 years of active ministry!

The Vision....

After the first printing of the book, <u>The Order of Melchizedek,</u> God gave me a vision of what He intended to do with this book around the world. But I know that God never does anything unless it is already finished. I knew that God was calling me to be part of manifesting here on earth a finished work from eternity-past concerning the supernatural establishment of <u>The Order of Melchizedek</u> on our troubled planet. In this vision, I saw myself standing on a map of the seven continents. Suddenly pockets of red lights began to appear on the seven continents. While I looked, a white beam of light began to join the red dots together, and suddenly, I saw it. A net or a matrix of red and white lights had covered the seven continents. I said to the Lord, "Lord what is this?"

The Answer...

"Son, the red lights are men and women whom I have been preparing to have a ministry that is patterned after the Order of Melchizedek. The white light that was connecting the red dots is the revelation that I have placed in your book. The revelation that I have given you will become the catalyst that will unite this global movement of my people who are waking up to the fact that I have called them to be "Kings and Priests" in the earth.

The Problem....

I was in Tulsa, Oklahoma, to meet with publishers who wanted to take the Order of Melchizedek nationwide and then worldwide. After a successful meeting with these potential investors, the Lord dropped a word into my spirit that put everything in perspective. He told me that He wanted to take this message around the world as He had promised me, but HE DID NOT WANT ME TO LIMIT HIM by thinking that I was going to single-handedly carry this very important message to the global Body of Christ. God told me that He wanted me to duplicate myself in other faithful men and women who can also teach others. The Lord said to me "Son, as this message explodes around the world you will start getting an abundance of ministry invitations; I do not want you to turn down invitations without giving my people an alternative minister" who can go and teach on the Order of Melchizedek in your absence." This instruction and conversation from the Lord weighed deeply upon my spirit!

The Confirmation...
A couple of hours after the Lord spoke to me, I got a phone call that made it clear that the Lord had spoken to me about duplicating myself so that the message on the Order of Melchizedek could spread beyond my capacity to travel. Two very astute businessmen from Northwest Arkansas called me, and this is what they told me, "Dr. Myles, we feel the message that God has given you will also become our life message, but even though we are very excited about it, we feel ill-equipped to teach it. We want to be able to explain the Order of Melchizedek with as much clarity and passion as you do. We would like to come and spend a weekend with you, so you can pour all that you have into our lives!" I was both speechless and excited! God had cornered me into a position of no retreat.

The Solution...
On my drive back from Tulsa, I prayed earnestly. During my time of prayer, the Holy Spirit gave me the solution. He told me, "Son, the spirit of a judge is upon you NOW! I have given you the power to "summon" my people from all walks of life to come and be "judged" concerning their understanding and compliance with the Order of Melchizedek. Call them NOW...and they will come.

The Birth of a Leadership Training Institute...
The Holy Spirit showed me how to set up a very intimate, prophetic, and intensive Training Institute that would train "Kingdom citizens, especially marketplace leaders" on how to operate under the Order of Melchizedek as "Kings and Priests." This intimate time of ministry and training will usually take place, one weekend a month. Students start class on Thursday and Graduate on Sunday. The name that the Holy Spirit gave me for this Supernatural School of Ministry is "The Order of Melchizedek Leadership University" (also known as The Order of Melchizedek Supernatural School of Ministry).

Tuition Fees....

"The Order of Melchizedek Leadership University or OMSSM" is NOT a tuition-based institute so there are NO tuition fees. Students simply pay a one-time $199 registration fee instead of $1700 if we charged the appropriate tuition fees for the 17 Modules we offer in the School. This registration fee will also be used to cover the student manual and graduation certificate. Those who register at the door will pay more. The only other expenses incurred if a student is from out of town are lodging, meals, and travel.

Offerings of Honor...
Since the Order of Melchizedek Leadership University is NOT a tuition-based institute, students are asked to come prayerful about sowing _Free Will_ "Offerings of Honor" into the life and ministry of the Chancellor before the Sunday morning graduation service.

The Alumni....
Graduating students will be given an opportunity to join the "Order of Melchizedek Alumni Association." This is an online community of "Melchizedeks" (men and women who are graduates of OMLU/OMSSM) who are operating as "Kings and Priests" both in the temple and in the marketplace. You will have an opportunity to create some significant relationships with men and women of like precious faith who are SOLD OUT to CHRIST!

Yours for Kingdom Advancement

Dr. Francis Myles
Chancellor

OM SCHOOL OF MINISTRY OBJECTIVES

- Transform ordinary believers into CMVP's = "Christ's Most Valuable Player" as they acquire a working knowledge of the Melchizedek priesthood.

- To create a platform for total transformation for men and women who are called to be "Josephs and Daniels" in the Marketplace.

- To train and raise an end-time dominion minded company of men and women who have a ministry that is patterned after the Order of Melchizedek (A King-priest Ministry).

- To train pastors who desire to ontroduce their congregation to the Order of Melchizedek.

- To CHANGE the WORLD...one person at a time!

Let's get started!

1. IN SEARCH OF VISION

Where there is no vision, the people perish: but he that keepeth the law, happy is he. (Proverbs 29:18)

REVIEW AND REFLECT:

Take a few moments to read the following nuggets of wisdom.

"Frustration with the Present Creates the Future" Mike Murdock
"The Flowers of Tomorrow are hidden in the Seeds of Today"...Unknown Philosopher
"Empty your wallet into your mind, and your mind will fill your wallet." Benjamin Franklin
"Jesus Christ is the Kingdom of God putting on Flesh and then Walking" Stanley E Jones

WHY SEARCH FOR YOUR VISION?

- Your vision is an image of the future that you desire that inspires you to work towards its fulfillment.
- Your vision inspires you to break away from your Comfort Zone into the faith world of the unknown.
- When you do not have a vision, you are easily distracted by every demonic scheme that is designed to rob you of your focus.
- Your vision is an essential portrait of your future.
- When you have a clear and well-defined vision, it informs all the decisions that you make.

Consider these facts...

- A vision engages your heart and your regenerated spirit
- A vision expresses your deepest desire for yourself and your loved ones
- A vision provides meaning to the Work or Study that you are doing
- A vision is the release of unexpressed desires or dreams
- A vision often expresses your desire for a more excellent standard of living and personal accomplishments.

Make your vision so powerful that each time you revisit it in your mind, you get deeply moved to an unshakeable course of action. We want you to create in a few minutes a clear cut vision of what you desire to accomplish in your life by taking this course.

EXPLORE AND ASSIMILATE:

Through the following exercises, you have the opportunity to create a vision for your life. We are going to ask you to take a few minutes to prayerfully meditate then answer the questions. These questions are designed to set your creative spirit free to DREAM and DREAM BIG. Go beyond your current life circumstances. See past what you are currently going through, and picture your ideal life in the Kingdom of God.

YOUR QUEST FOR VISION:

Please answer the following questions:

1. What would I do in my life, if I knew that I could never fail?

_____

_____

_____

2. At the end of my life; what will be my greatest accomplishment?

_____

_____

_____

_____

3. What mission in life absolutely inspires me to action?

_____

_____

_____

_____

4. What are I am going to do to change the world with my understanding of the Order of Melchizedek?

_____

_____

_____

_____

5. What work do I find absorbing and engaging?

_____

_____

_____

_____

2. FINDING YOUR "BIG WHY"

REVIEW AND REFLECT

The purpose of this section is to help you ESTABLISH three critical things before going through the course.

1. We want to help you CONNECT with your "BIG WHY"
2. We want to help you DEFINE your CORE BELIEFS
3. We want to help you HONOR your VISION and PURPOSE for coming to the Order of Melchizedek Leadership University weekend encounter.

WHY DISCOVER YOUR BIG WHY

Your "Big Why" is your deep, emotional, and spiritual reason for wanting to enhance your walk with God by attending the Order of Melchizedek Leadership University weekend encounter. Your "Big Why" connects your presence for being in this class to your life vision. Your "Big Why" is your connection to what God desires to do with you to advance His Kingdom here on earth. Your "Big Why" motivates you to achieve your goals and dreams.

When you know your "Big Why" for attending the Order of Melchizedek Leadership University weekend encounter, you will easily stay on track during the rest of this weekend. Without a "Big Why"- you will lack a clear vision of how graduating from the Order of Melchizedek Leadership University contributes to the building of the life that you have desired for yourself. When you are aware of your "Big Why," you make better choices every day and can stay the course. You will expend your energy developing the kind of relationships and businesses that make your heart sing and shout!

Module ONE

THE GREAT TRANSITION: FROM INSTITUTIONAL CHRISTIANITY TO THE KINGDOM

And when he had found him, he brought him unto Antioch. And it came to pass, that a whole year they assembled themselves with the church, and taught much people. And the disciples were called Christians first in Antioch. (Acts 11:26)

Module OVERVIEW:

In this module, we will answer the following questions:

1. What is the difference between _____ and the Kingdom?

2. What are _____ ?

3. What are the unintended consequences of Emperor Constantine's _____

   of Christianity?

4. Why the _____ of our time is the transition from

   institutional Christianity to the Kingdom.

Important points to remember on this module:

- The spiritual and mental fortitude needed to make the transition from Institutional Christianity to the Kingdom
- The two classes of Christians within the Christian religion (Nominal and Committed)
- The roots and origins of the widespread divisions within the Christian religion
- How doctrinal chambers of containment work and how they give birth to spiritual subcultures that compete with Kingdom culture
- The thirteen theological systems that have mushroomed within the Christian religion
- Christianity in the light of history and rise of anti-Semitism
- The influence of Emperor Constantine on the Christian religion
- The power and technology of tames and how it relates to the name "Christians"

STUDENT NOTES:

_____

_____

_____

_____

_____

_____

_____

_____

_____

_____

_____

_____

_____

_____

_____

_____

_____

_____

_____

_____

_____

_____

_____

_____

_____

_____

_____

_____

_____

_____

Module TWO

IS JESUS MELCHIZEDEK?

Melchizedek: *"Without father or mother, without genealogy, without beginning of days or end of life, like the Son of God he remains a priest forever."* (Hebrews 7:3)

Jesus: *"The beginning of the Gospel about Jesus Christ, the Son of God."* (Mark 1:1)

Module OVERVIEW:

In this module we will answer the following questions:

1. What is the _____ of the Melchizedek who met Abram in the valley?

2. What are the _____ between Melchizedek and Jesus?

3. What are the three _____ who are addressed by the title "Son of God?"

4. Is _____ Melchizedek?

5. What is the _____ of Melchizedek?

Important Points to remember on this module:

- Schools of thought on the identity of Melchizedek
- Why Adam is NOT Melchizedek
- Why Shem is NOT Melchizedek
- The identical characteristics between Yeshua and Melchizedek
- The Dead Sea Scrolls references to Melchizedek

STUDENT NOTES:

_____

_____

_____

_____

_____

_____

_____

_____

_____

_____

_____

_____

_____

_____

_____

_____

_____

_____

_____

_____

_____

_____

_____

_____

_____

_____

_____

Module THREE

UNDERSTANDING THE KINGDOM THROUGH KINGNEBUCHANEDZZER'S VISION

"In your vision, Your Majesty, you saw standing before you a huge, shining statue of a man. It was a frightening sight. 32 The head of the statue was made of fine gold. Its chest and arms were silver, its belly and thighs were bronze, 33 its legs were iron, and its feet were a combination of iron and baked clay. 34 As you watched, a rock was cut from a mountain, but not by human hands. It struck the feet of iron and clay, smashing them to bits. 35 The whole statue was crushed into small pieces of iron, clay, bronze, silver, and gold. Then the wind blew them away without a trace, like chaff on a threshing floor. But the rock that knocked the statue down became a great mountain that covered the whole earth. Daniel 2:31-35

Module OVERVIEW:

In this module, we will answer the following questions:

1. How did the _____ subjugate conquered peoples and territories?

2. What is the Prophetic Implication of King Nebuchadnezzar's Vision of the _____
   _____ ?

3. Why did God plant the _____ in Babylon?

4. We will examine the message of the   _____

Important points to remember on this module:

- Understand the Kingdom of God through King Nebuchadnezzar's vision
- Examine the nature and inner workings of Kingdoms
- Examine Christ as God's Pattern Son
- Examine the prophetic implications of King's Nebuchadnezzar's vision of the golden image
- Examine the concept of colonization
- Examine concept of the Kingdom now and its coming
- Examine the emerging Kingdom culture

STUDENT NOTES:

_____

_____

_____

_____

_____

_____

_____

_____

_____

_____

_____

_____

_____

_____

_____

_____

_____

_____

_____

_____

_____

_____

_____

_____

_____

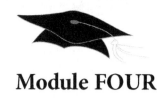

Module FOUR

THE ORDER OF FIRST THINGS

But seek ye first the kingdom of God, and his righteousness; and all these things shall be added unto you. Matthew 6:33

Module OVERVIEW:

In this module, we will answer the following questions:

1. What are _____ ?

2. What is the Order of _____ ?

3. What are the _____ that belong to the "Order of First?

Important points to remember about this module:

- The benefits of keeping the "Order of First Things"
- The perils of failing to "Keep the Order of First Things"
- How understanding roots and origins changes your life?

STUDENT NOTES:

_____

_____

_____

_____

_____

_____

_____

_____

_____

_____

_____

_____

_____

_____

_____

_____

_____

_____

_____

_____

_____

_____

_____

_____

_____

_____

_____

_____

_____

Module FIVE

REBUILDING THE TABERNACLE OF DAVID

*After this I will return, and will build again the **tabernacle** of **David**, which is fallen down; and I will build again the ruins thereof, and I will set it up: (Acts 15:16)*

Module OVERVIEW:

In this module, we will answer the following questions:

1. What is the _____ ?

2. What can we learn about the _____ of the Order of Melchizedek from David's Life?

3. How did _____ discover the Order of Melchizedek?

Important points to remember on this module:

- David's early years and their impact on his life
- The three spiritual and historical figures that God used to reveal to us the Order of Melchizedek and its inner workings
- David's behavior at Ziklag when his city was burnt to the ground and how it helps us to understand the Order of Melchizedek
- The power of the order of worship in David's life
- David's rise as a worshipping warrior
- The birth of Davidic type of churches and believers through the Order of Melchizedek
- David as the "man after God's own heart"
- The prophetic implications of the death of Uzziah
- How David discovered the Order of Melchizedek
- The Tabernacle of David and its inner workings

STUDENT NOTES:

_____

_____

_____

_____

_____

_____

_____

_____

_____

_____

_____

_____

_____

_____

_____

_____

_____

_____

_____

_____

_____

_____

_____

_____

_____

_____

_____

_____

_____

_____

_____

_____

Module SIX

AN INDEPTH ANALYSIS OF ABRAHAM'S MEETING WITH MELCHIZEDEK

After Abram returned from his victory over Kedorlaomer and all his allies, the king of Sodom went out to meet him in the valley of Shaveh (that is, the King's Valley).18 And Melchizedek, the King of Salem and a priest of God Most High, brought Abram some bread and wine. (Genesis 14:17-18)

Module OVERVIEW:

In this module we will answer the following questions:

1. What were the _____ of Abram's Faith Promise?

2. What is the _____ of the Melchizedek who met Abram in the Valley of the Kings?

3. What is real _____?

4. Why did Melchizedek _____ Abram in the Valley of the Kings?

Important points to remember about this module:

- The call of Abram and its prophetic implications
- The terms and conditions of Abram's faith promise
- Abram's demonically engineered panic during a time of severe economic recession
- The prophetic implications of Abram's broken covenant with Sarah at the border of Egypt
- Abram's deceptive business practice in Egypt
- The poison of mixed blessings; "Snakes in Money Bags"
- Abram's greatest embarrassment; The dynamics of real Kingdom wealth
- Schools of thought on the identity of Melchizedek
- The prophetic implications of Abram's changed name

STUDENT NOTES:

_____
_____
_____
_____
_____
_____
_____
_____
_____
_____
_____
_____
_____
_____
_____
_____
_____
_____
_____
_____
_____
_____
_____
_____
_____
_____
_____

Module SEVEN

THE KING OF SODOM AND THE PERVESITY OF THIS PRESENT AGE

After Abram returned from his victory over Kedorlaomer and all his allies, the king of Sodom went out to meet him in the valley of Shaveh (that is, the King's Valley). (Genesis 14:17)

Module OVERVIEW:

In this module we will answer the following questions:

1. What is the Principle of _____?

2. What is the Demonic _____ System?

3. What does the _____ represent prophetically?

Important points to remember on this module:

- How the Order of Melchizedek is designed to deliver us from being corrupted by the demonic sodomic system
- The principle of perversity that is inherent in all man-made institutions
- What the king of Sodom represents prophetically; a snapshot of the underlying essence of this demonic sodomic system
- How the Order of Melchizedek can empower us to live above the power of the King of Sodom
- The prophetic implications of Lot's decision to move to Sodom
- How the demonic sodomic system can cause us to fight on the losing side
- The Order of Melchizedek and the technology of divine interception
- The dangers of doing business with the King of Sodom
- The reasons why Abram refused to take money from the King of Sodom
- Why many people end up with snakes in money bags

STUDENT NOTES:

_____
_____
_____
_____
_____
_____
_____
_____
_____
_____
_____
_____
_____
_____
_____
_____
_____
_____
_____
_____
_____
_____
_____
_____
_____

Module EIGHT

AN INDEPTH ANALYSIS OF THE BREAD AND WINE OF THE MELCHIZEDEK ORDER

And Melchizedek, the king of Salem and a priest of God Most High, brought Abram some bread and wine. Melchizedek blessed Abram with this blessing: "Blessed be Abram by God Most High, Creator of heaven and earth. (Genesis 14:18-19)

Module OVERVIEW:

In this module we will answer the following questions:

1. What is the Prophetic Significance of _____ that Melchizedek gave to Abram?

2. What is the Prophetic Significance of _____ that Melchizedek gave to Abram?

3. How does this _____ between Abram and Melchizedek affect us today?

Important points to remember on this module:

- The prophetic symbolism of the bread of the Melchizedek Order
- The prophetic symbolism of the wine of the Melchizedek Order
- The present-day benefits of the Sacrament of Holy Communion
- The prophetic implications of the Last Supper
- How to live above the dictates of the five senses

STUDENT NOTES:

_____

_____

_____

_____

_____

_____

_____

_____

_____

_____

_____

_____

_____

_____

_____

_____

_____

_____

_____

_____

_____

_____

_____

_____

_____

_____

Module NINE

AN INDEPTH ANALYSIS OF
THE ORDER OF MELCHIZEDEK

The Lord has taken an oath and will not break his vow: "You are a priest forever in the order of Melchizedek" (Psalm 110:4).

Module OVERVIEW:

In this module, we will answer the following questions:

1. Why is the Order of Melchizedek _____?

2. What is the_____?

3. What are the _____ of the Order of Melchizedek?

4. How_____ and position as the High Priest over the Order

   of Melchizedek affects_____?

Important points you should remember on this module:

- Paul's apologetic discourse on the Order of Melchizedek to the Hebrews
- The present-day prophetic implications of rediscovering the Order of Melchizedek
- The Doctrine of Christ, Sin and the Devil
- The superiority of the Order of Melchizedek over the Levitical Priesthood
- The spiritual currency of operating in the economy of the Kingdom
  under the Order of Melchizedek

STUDENT NOTES:

_____
_____
_____
_____
_____
_____
_____
_____
_____
_____
_____
_____
_____
_____
_____
_____
_____
_____
_____
_____
_____
_____
_____
_____
_____

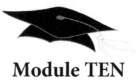

Module TEN

UNDERSTANDING YOUR INHERITANCE AS ABRAHAM'S STAR SEED

I will certainly bless you. I will multiply your descendants beyond number, like the stars in the sky and the sand on the seashore. Your descendants will conquer the cities of their enemies (Genesis 22:17)

Module OVERVIEW:

In this module, we will answer the following questions:

1. Who is the_____?

2. What are the_____ that God gave to Abraham?

3. Who is Abraham's _____ ?

Important points to remember on this module:

:

- Abraham's Covenant of Total Obedience
- The prophetic implications of the birth of Isaac
- The prophetic implications of the offering of Isaac on Mount Moriah
- The meaning of the place called "Jehovah Jireh"
- The spiritual inheritance of Abraham's SAND and STAR seeds

STUDENT NOTES

_____
_____
_____
_____
_____
_____
_____
_____
_____
_____
_____
_____
_____
_____
_____
_____
_____
_____
_____
_____
_____
_____
_____
_____
_____
_____
_____
_____
_____
_____

Module ELEVEN

THE MANIFEST SONS OF GOD

For the earnest expectation of the creation eagerly waits for the revealing of the sons of God. For the creation was subjected to futility, not willingly, but because of Him who subjected it in hope; because the creation itself also will be delivered from the bondage of corruption into the glorious liberty of the children of God. For we know that the whole creation groans and labors with birth pangs together until now. (Romans 8:19-22 NKJV)

Module OVERVIEW:

In this module, we will answer the following questions:

1. What is God's "_____?"

2. Why is all of creation groaning for the _____ of the sons of God?

3. What is the prophetic implications of the _____ of Christ?

4. What is the _____ between the Order of Melchizedek and the manifest sons of God?

Important points to remember on this module:

- God's Big Idea
- Man's dominion mandate
- The prophetic implications of the fall of man
- How understanding the dichotomy of Jesus Christ impacts race relations between members of the Body of Christ
- The ministry of the manifest sons of God

Module TWELVE

THE FATHERING DIMENSION

Look, I am sending you the prophet Elijah before the great and dreadful day of the Lord arrives. His preaching will turn the hearts of fathers to their children, and the hearts of children to their fathers. Otherwise I will come and strike the land with a curse. (Malachi 4:5-6)

For even if you were to have ten thousand teachers [to guide you] in Christ, yet you would not have many fathers [who led you to Christ and assumed responsibility for you], for I became your father in Christ Jesus through the good news [of salvation]. 1 Corinthians 4:15

Module OVERVIEW:

In this module, we will answer the following questions:

1. What is the "_____?"

2. What is an _____ , and how is it impacting the destiny of Nations?

3. What _____ was Joseph operating under when he was in Egypt?

4. What _____ did Joseph hold in Egypt?

5. Why Did God give Joseph so _____ with Pharaoh?

6. Why is God raising a _____ the nations of the world?

Important points to remember about the Module:

- The prophetic implications of Malachi 4:5-6
- The symptoms of an Orphan Spirit and its practical implications
- The fall of Lucifer and his angelic host
- How to become a "Father of many nations"
- The Joseph mantle and mandate
- How to transform the marketplace and our culture

STUDENT NOTES

_____
_____
_____
_____
_____
_____
_____
_____
_____
_____
_____
_____
_____
_____
_____
_____
_____
_____
_____
_____
_____
_____
_____
_____
_____
_____

_____

_____

_____

_____

_____

_____

_____

_____

_____

_____

_____

_____

_____

_____

_____

_____

_____

_____

_____

_____

_____

_____

_____

_____

_____

_____

Module THIRTEEN

TAKING CHRIST AND HIS KINGDOM INTO THE MARKETPLACE

And when he had found him, he brought him unto Antioch. And it came to pass, that a whole year they assembled themselves with the church, and taught much people. And the disciples were called Christians first in Antioch. (Acts 11:26)

And it came to pass, as we went to prayer, a certain damsel possessed with a spirit of divination met us, which brought her masters much gain by soothsaying: The same followed Paul and us, and cried, saying, These men are the servants of the most high God, which shew unto us the way of salvation. And this did she many days. But Paul, being grieved, turned and said to the spirit, I command thee in the name of Jesus Christ to come out of her. And he came out the same hour. And when he masters saw that the hope of their gains was gone, they caught Paul and Silas, and drew them into the market place unto the rulers, And brought them to the magistrates, saying, These men, being Jews, do exceedingly trouble our city. (Acts 16:16-20 KJV)

Module OVERVIEW:

1. What is the _____ within the context of Scripture?

2. How will the Order of Melchizedek help the Church to _____

   and His Kingdom into the Marketplace?

3. Why is the Marketplace _____ for the Cultural war

   between the Kingdom of God and the Kingdom of Darkness?

Important points to remember:

- The primary difference between the Levitical priesthood and the Order of Melchizedek
- Why many churches are trapped in a Levitical mindset
- God's Kingdom agenda for the Marketplace
- The King-Priest leadership paradigm

37

Module FOURTEEN

THE ORDER OF MELCHIZEDEK AND THE 7 MOUNTAINS OF CULTURE

Then the seventh angel sounded: And there were loud voices in heaven, saying, "The kingdoms of this world have become the kingdoms of our Lord and of His Christ, and He shall reign forever and ever!" Revelation 11:15 (NKJV)

And here is the mind which hath wisdom. The seven heads are seven mountains, on which the woman sitteth. 10 And there are seven kings: five are fallen, and one is, and the other is not yet come; and when he cometh, he must continue a short space. Revelation 17:9-10

*And David said unto Ahimelech, And is there not here under thine hand spear or sword? for I have neither brought my sword nor my weapons with me, because the king's **business** required haste. (1 Samuel 21:8)*

*Seest thou a man diligent in his **business**? he shall stand before kings; he shall not stand before mean men. Proverbs 22:29*

Module OVERVIEW:

1. What are the _____ of Babylonian (Culture)?

2. What is the Prophetic Interpretation of _____ Babylon the Great?

3. How will the Order of Melchizedek help _____ the Seven Mountains of Culture?

4. What is the _____ ?

5. How can the Order of Melchizedek help entrepreneurs _____ in their vehicle of commerce?

Important points to remember on this module:

- The impact that the Order of Melchizedek can have on the growth and profitability of any business
- How to transform any business into a Kingdom business
- The prophetic implications of inviting the Lordship of Christ in your vehicle of commerce
- Demonic attacks on Kingdom entrepreneurs
- The importance of the principle of rest in the Mountain of Business
- The importance of discovering the Mountain Kingdom, God has called you to!

STUDENT NOTES

Module FIFTEEN

TITHING UNDER THE ORDER OF MELCHIZEDEK

And blessed be God Most High, who has defeated your enemies for you." Then Abram gave Melchizedek a tenth of all the goods he had recovered (Genesis 14:20).

Module OVERVIEW:

In this module, we will answer the following questions:

1. What is the difference between tithing under the _____ and the Order of Melchizedek?

2. Why tithing into the Order of Melchizedek is the _____ of tithing known to man?

3. Why did Abraham compare tithing to the " _____ "?

4. Why the popular Malachi 3 tithing system is _____ tithing system for New Testament believers?

Important points to remember on this module:

- The benefits of tithing under the Levitical Priesthood
- The benefits of tithing under the Order of Melchizedek Priesthood
- Why you are NOT cursed for not giving tithes
- Why the word "window" does not appear in the New Testament as a "Covenantal Blessing"
- Money is the lowest asset in the Kingdom economy
- Divine Interception is the most important benefit of Tithing under the Order of Melchizedek

STUDENT NOTES

Module SIXTEEN

A PRIEST ON HIS THRONE

Now of the things which we have spoken this is the sum: We have such an high priest, who is set on the right hand of the throne of the Majesty in the heavens; (Hebrews 8:1)

Yes, [you are building a temple of the Lord, but] it is He Who shall build the [true] temple of the Lord, and He shall bear the honor and glory [as of the only begotten of the Father] and shall sit and rule upon His throne. And He shall be a Priest upon His throne, and the counsel of peace shall be between the two [offices—Priest and King]. (Zechariah 6:13.Amplified)

Module OVERVIEW:

In this module, we will answer the following questions:

1. What was_____ of the Prophet Zechariah?

2. What is the Babylonian _____

3. Why a Levitical _____ separates the Temple from the Marketplace?

4. What's holding up the supernatural _____ ?

Important points to remember on this module:

- The connection between the Order of Melchizedek and the end-time wealth transfer
- The absence of a royal lineage in the Levitical priesthood
- The mystery of Babylon the Great
- Why material prosperity is important to advancing the Kingdom

Module SEVENTEEN

BREAKING GENERATIONAL CURSES UNDER THE ORDER OF MELCHIZEDEK

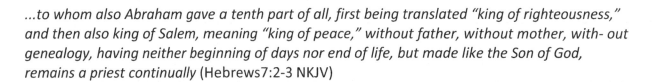

...to whom also Abraham gave a tenth part of all, first being translated "king of righteousness," and then also king of Salem, meaning "king of peace," without father, without mother, with- out genealogy, having neither beginning of days nor end of life, but made like the Son of God, remains a priest continually (Hebrews7:2-3 NKJV)

Then God gave the people all these instructions "I am the Lord your God, who rescued you from the land of Egypt, the place of your slavery. "You must not have any other god but me. "You must not make for yourself an idol of any kind or an image of anything in the heavens or on the earth or in the sea. You must not bow down to them or worship them, for I, the Lord your God, am a jealous God who will not tolerate your affection for any other gods. I lay the sins of the parents upon their children; the entire family is affected—even children in the third and fourth generations of those who reject me. (Exodus 20:1-5)

Module OVERVIEW:

In this module, we will answer the following questions:

1. What is a _____ Curse?

2. What is _____?

3. How can the Order of Melchizedek help us _____ of generational curses once and for all?

4. What is _____ the Bloodline?

Important points on this module:

- How inheritance law affects us in the area of generational curses
- The power of bloodlines or lineages
- The prophetic implications of the absence of genealogy in the Melchizedek priesthood
- The prophetic symbolism of "Jumping the Line!"

STUDENT NOTES

_____
_____
_____
_____
_____
_____
_____
_____
_____
_____
_____
_____
_____
_____
_____
_____
_____
_____
_____
_____
_____
_____
_____
_____

ANSWER KEY SECTION:

Module 1: Answers to the Questions:
1. Institutional Christianity
2. Spiritual Subcultures
3. Nationalization
4. Greatest Transition

Module 2: Answers to the Questions:
1. Identity
2. Identical Characteristics
3. Individuals
4. Jesus
5. Order of

Module 3: Answers to the Questions:
1. Babylonians
2. Golden Image
3. Four Hebrew Boys
4. The Gospel of the Kingdom

Module 4: Answers to the Questions:
1. Roots and Origins
2. First Things
3. Things

Module 5: Answers to the Questions:
1. Tabernacle of David
2. Inner Workings
3. King David

Module 6: Answer to the Questions:
1. Conditions
2. Prophetic Identity
3. Kingdom Wealth
4. Intercept

Module 7: Answers to the Questions:
1. Perversity
2. Sodomic
3. King of Sodom

Module 8: Answers to the Questions:
1. Heavenly Bread
2. Heavenly Wine
3. Covenant Exchange

Module 9: Answers to the Questions:
1. An Order
2. The Order of Melchizedek
3. Inner Workings
4. Christ Person, Kingdom Citizens

Module 10: Answers to the Questions:
1. Sand Seed of Abraham
2. Two Brands
3. Star Seed

Module 11: Answers to the Questions:
1. Big Idea
2. The Manifestation
3. Dichotomy
4. Spiritual Connection

Module 12: Answers to the Questions:
1. Fathering Spirit
2. Orphan Spirit
3. Order
4. Favor
5. Cooperate Joseph

ANSWER KEY SECTION:

Module 13: Answers to the Questions:
1. Marketplace
2. Take Christ, Kingdom
3. The Ultimate Battle Ground, This World

Module 14: Answers to the Questions:
1. Seven Mountains
2. The Demonic System
3. Kingdom Citizens
4. Mountain of Business
5. Prosper

Module 15: Answers to the Questions:
1. Levitical Order
2. Highest Form
3. Lifting of hands
4. Malachi
5. Not the Best
6. Money

Module 16: Answers to the Questi
1. The Prophetic Vision
2. Demonic System
3. Supernatural Transfer
4. Mindset

Module 17: Answers to the Questi
1. Generational Curse
2. Genetic Salvation
3. Break Free
4. Jumping the Line

Made in the USA
Las Vegas, NV
11 November 2020